Federico Federici

A Private Notebook Of Winds

LN
libri della neve

A private notebook of winds
All rights reserved
© Federico Federici 2019
ISBN 9798640410952
http://federicofederici.net
http://leserpent.wordpress.com

libri della neve
PRINTED ON EARTH

The original of this book belongs to the Academy of Fine Arts Palermo artists' book collection.

wind-learning
machine

a private
notebook
of winds

Federico
Federici

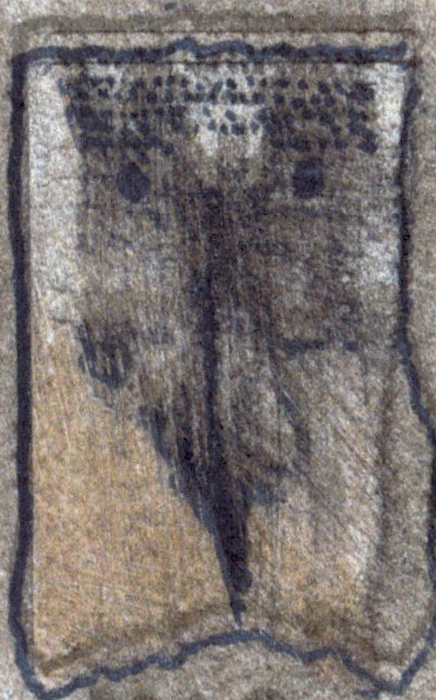

2019

collected on Earth
Federico Federici - 2019

A PRIVATE NOTEBOOK OF WINDS

FEDERICO FEDERICI

(collected on Earth)

Spring determines complete phase incoherence
sometime: leaves pulse in the noise of the movement

ensued from redundant wind, the density
of air drops among tall firs, beech trees and oaks.

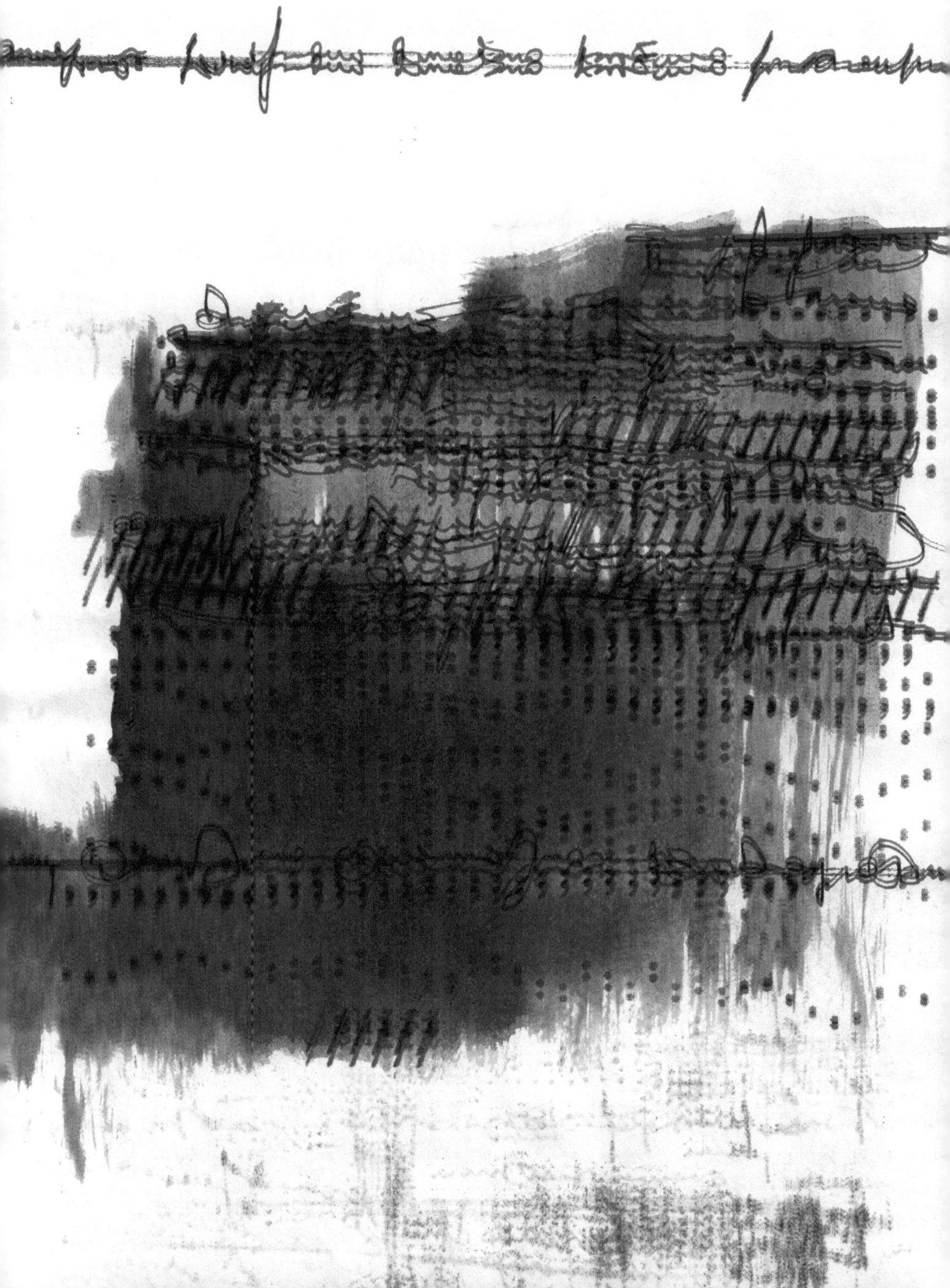

Seeming continuous variables such as barks, membranes or surfacing root hairs get observed under flickering leaves at the discrete times of the wind spikes. This description requires us to infer the pattern of hidden variables while we observe only a sparse number of them.

The mathematics of the woods
severs vibrating needles.

    inked dark
    linked ark
    inked bark
    inked axe

reckons outspread leaves, weighs the
perennial leafing of ache

in the fresh echoes of wind,
the light pressure, that of dead

twigs, the shards of resinous
words, the hewn patterns of runes,

A   I   R
DENSITY
some numbers and all their rules.

The wind is a set of continuous statements whose size is (unknown) It equates with a brain.

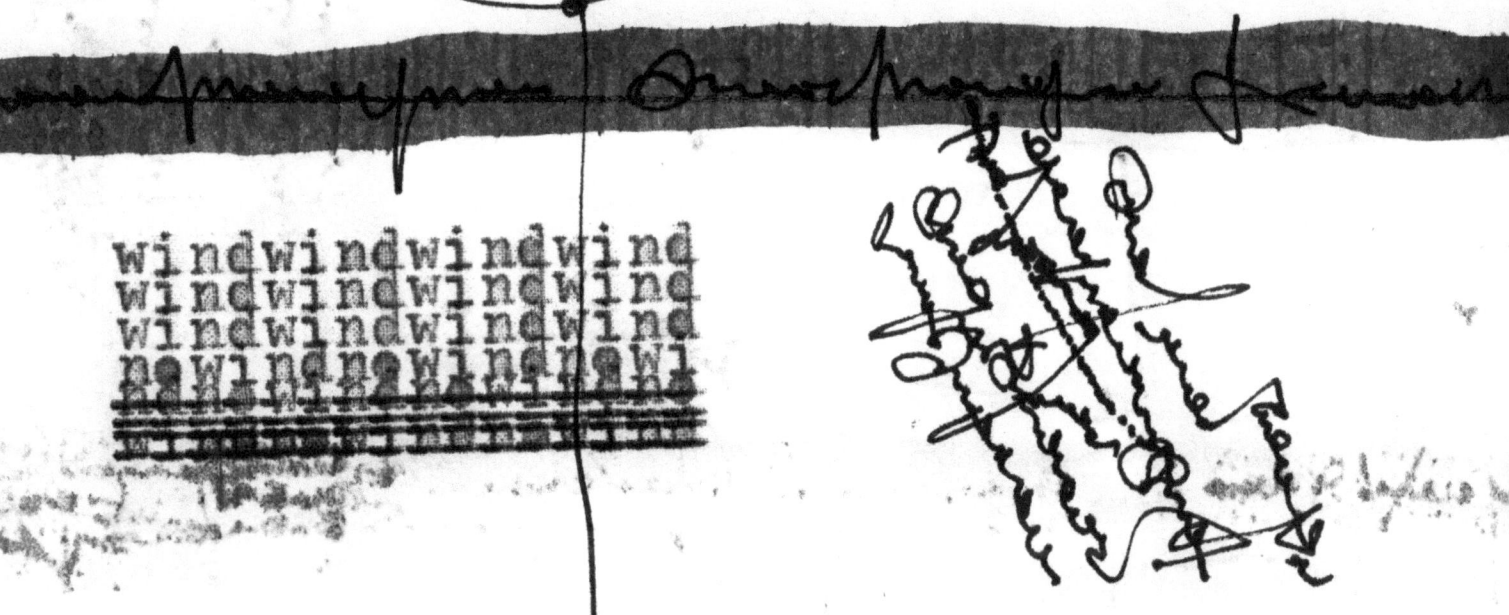

The vast number of variables the movements of the (woods) consist of is intractable.

Nor do we know how to solve the wind, a plot of which may (converge) to a particular loop.

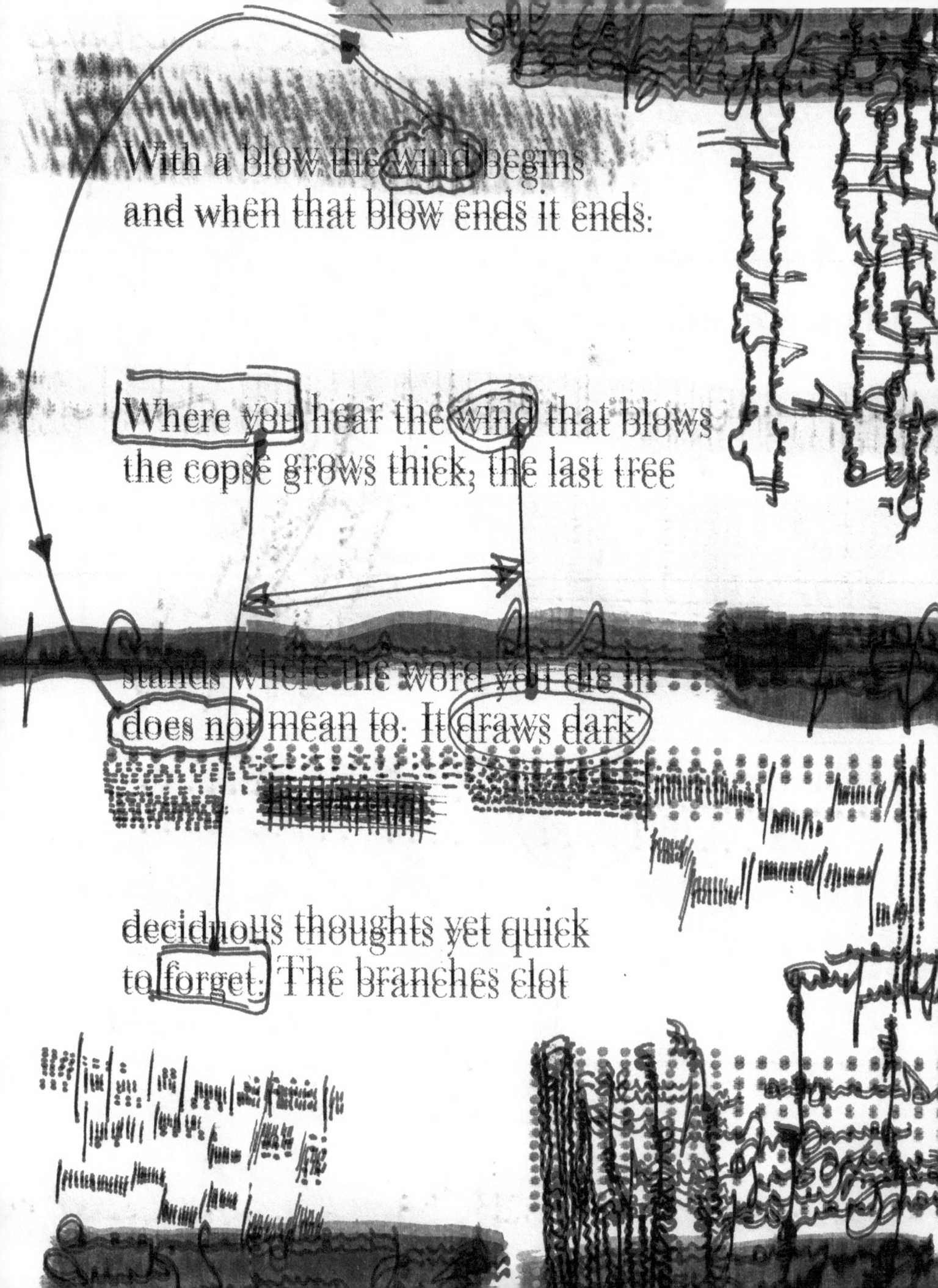

With a blow the wind begins
and when that blow ends it ends:

Where you hear the wind that blows
the copse grows thick; the last tree

stands where the word you used in
does not mean to. It draws dark

deciduous thoughts yet quick
to forget. The branches clot

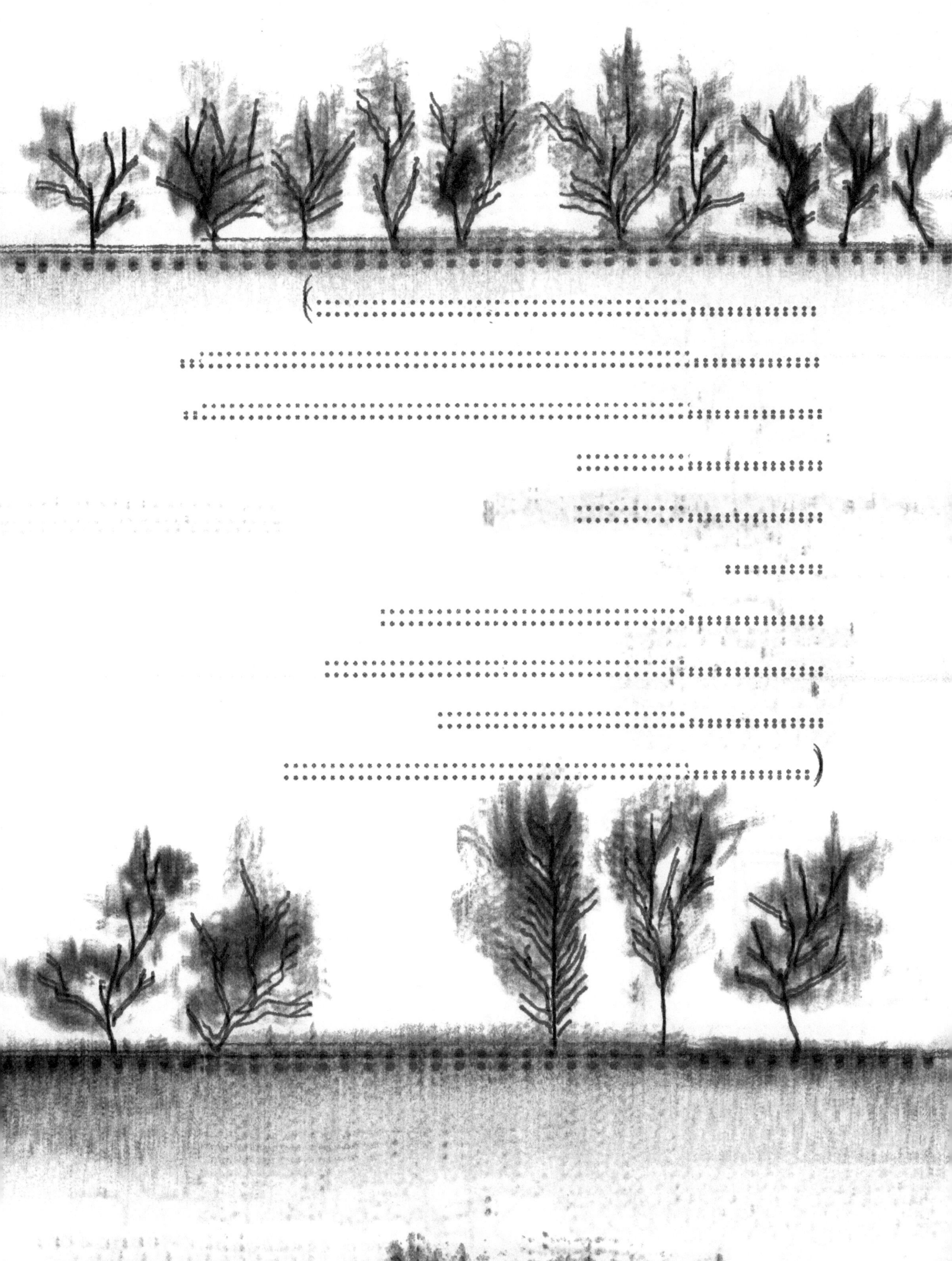

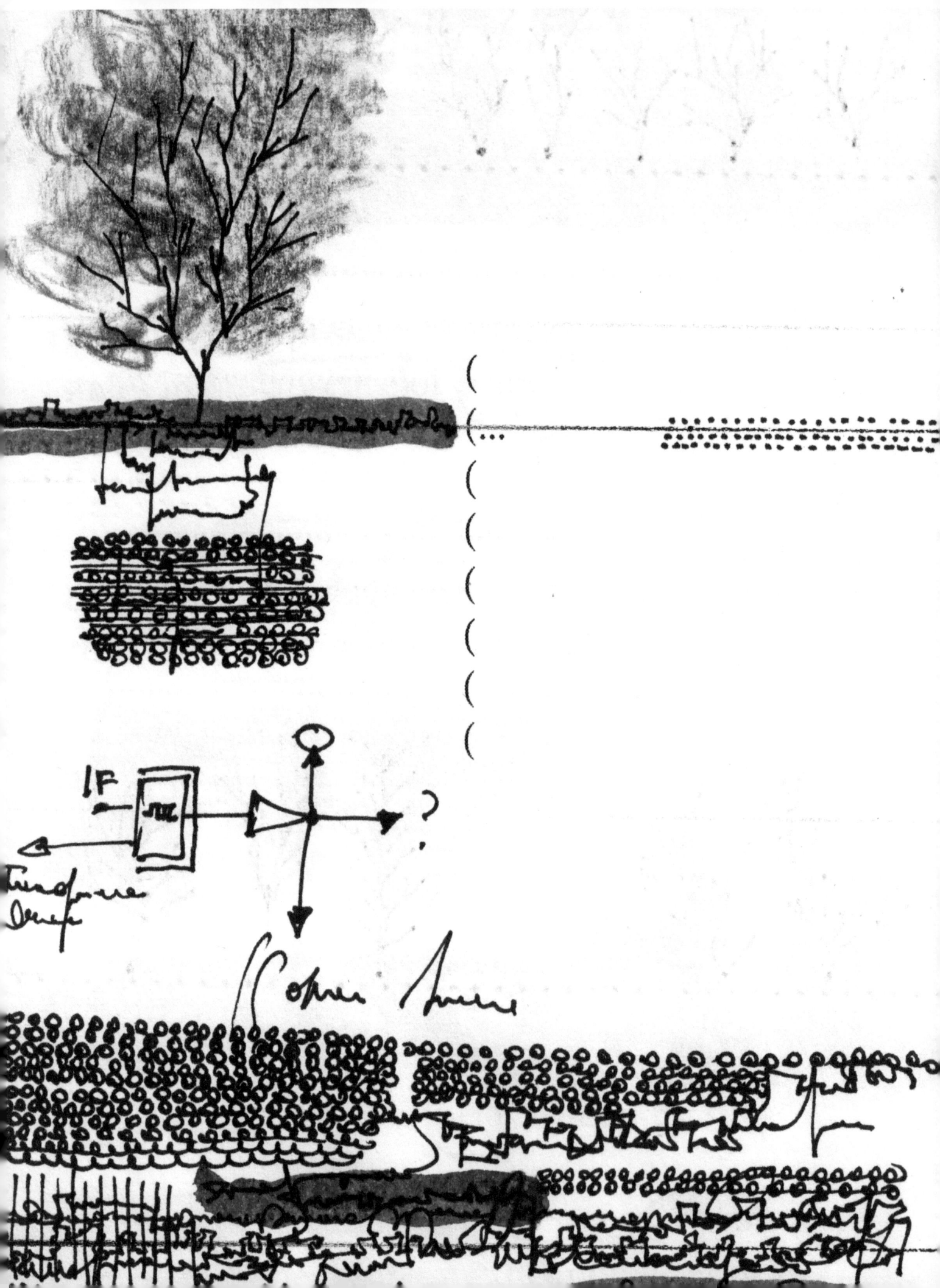

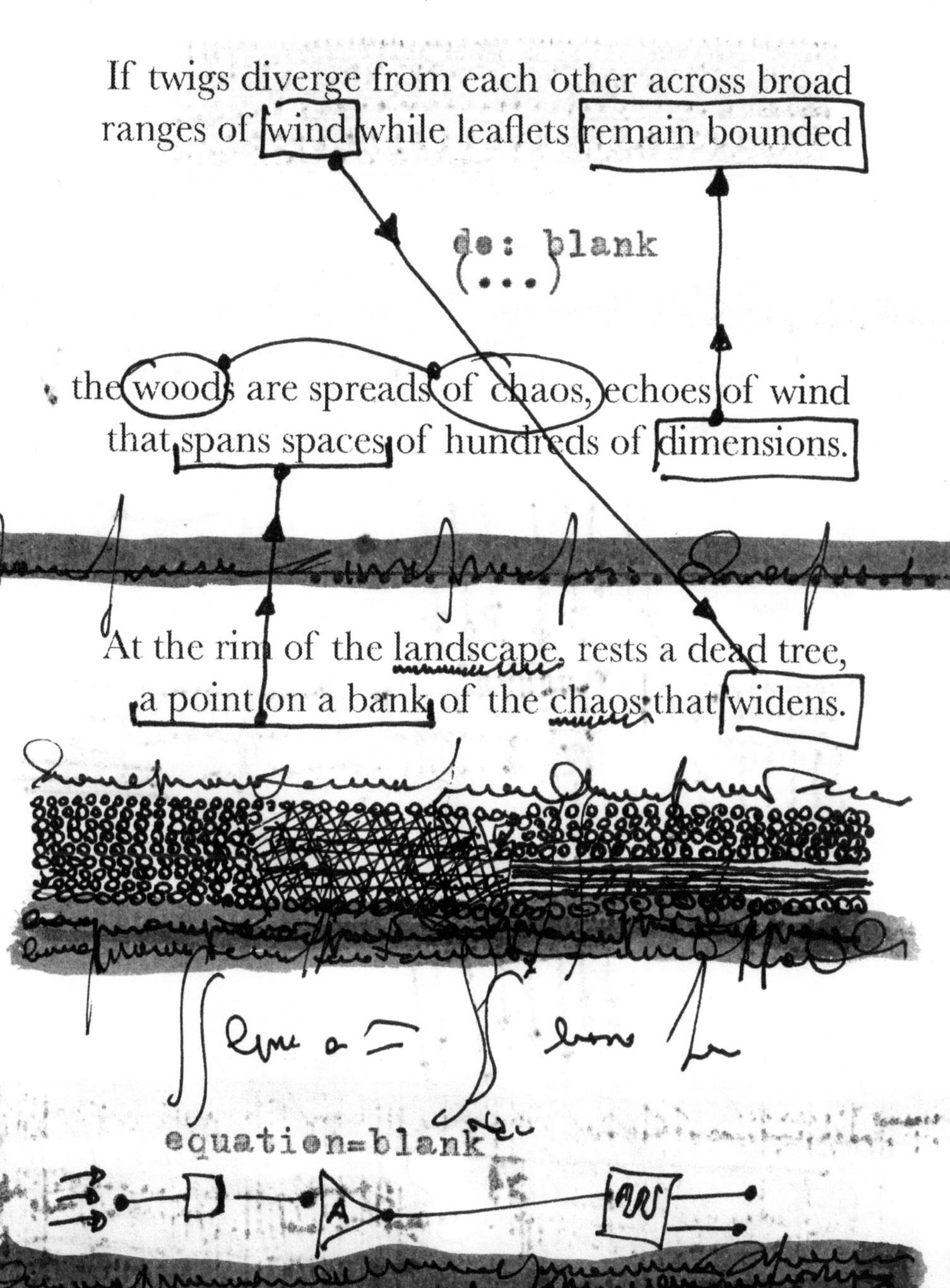

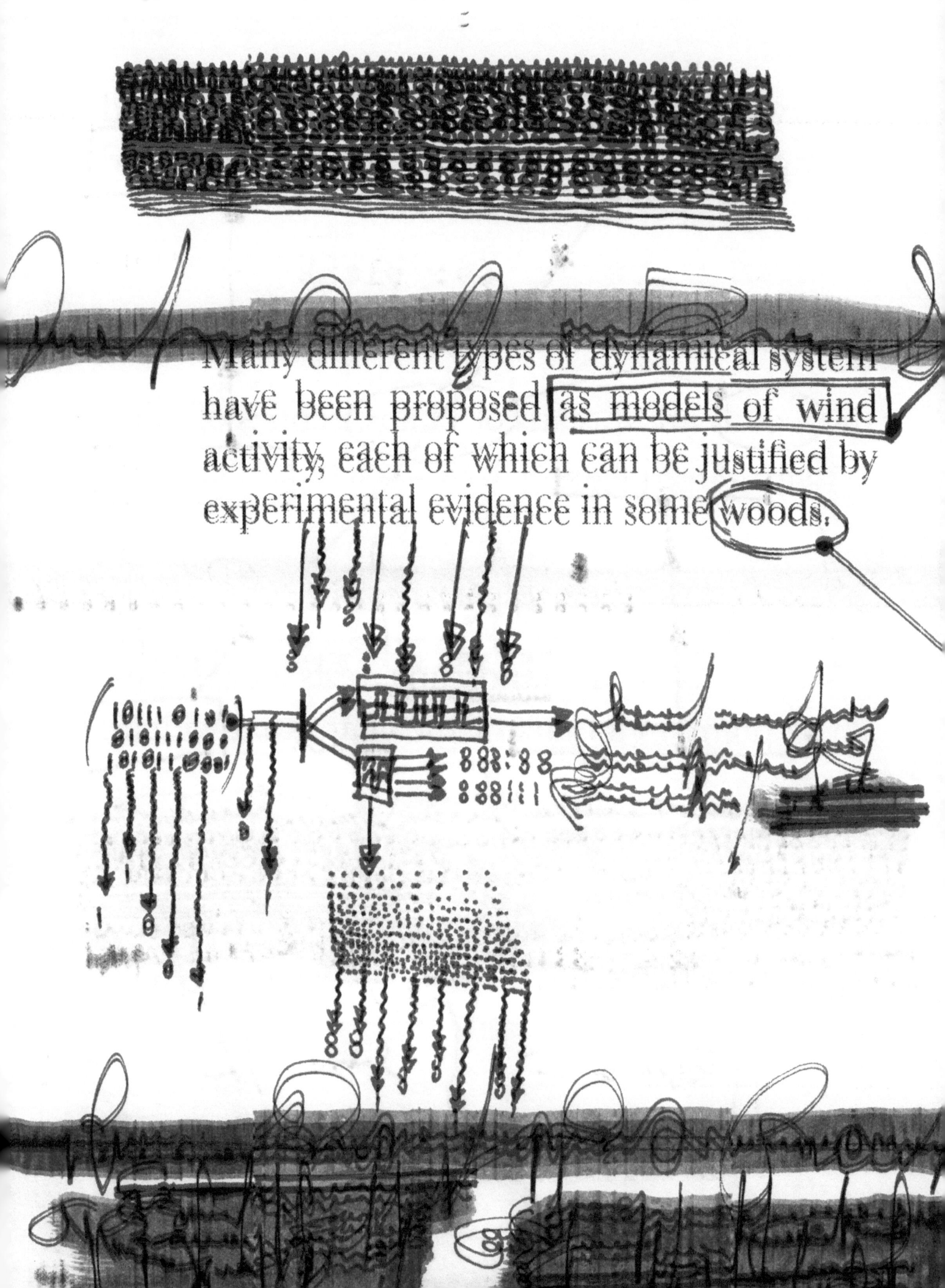

Many different types of dynamical system have been proposed as models of wind activity, each of which can be justified by experimental evidence in some woods.

Temperature fluctuations set the principle of memory formation and retrieval.

Regions of cortex and sapwood operate in terms of

The wind's steady-state firing rate; the transient of resinous air over the slope of firs.

Equally spaced needles resonate. Cycles of slow tilting loops plot diagrams of the woods.

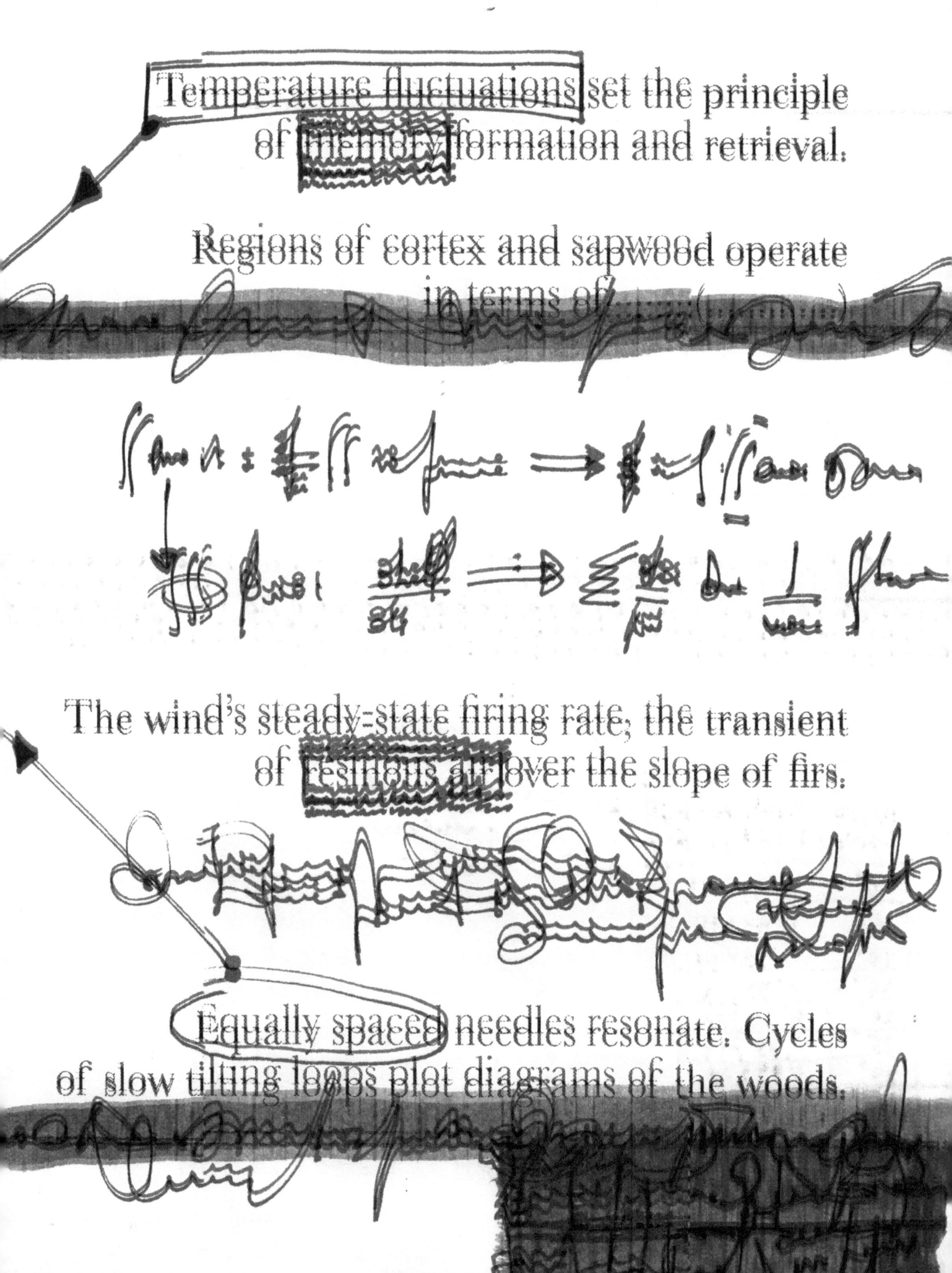

```
0010010010010000100101000101001000100 0100
01101011101010101110101011100100010010110001010
001010100001000010101101101101010010100100010
0010101010010011100100100111001010010010010
```

TEMPE-RATUR	GEWICHT VON 1 CC H$_2$O IN g
0°	0.99988
5°	0.99999
10°	0.99974
15°	0.99915
20°	0.99827
25°	0.99714
30°	0.99577
35°	0.99417
40°	0.99236
45°	0.99035
50°	0.98817

0/00/0/0/0/00/0/00/0/00/0/00
000/111/010/010/0/00/00/0/00
0/0100/0/000/1/00/00/000
0/00/0010/0/000/1/00/00

blank
trace
blank
tense black
trace

When woods possess multiple point attractor states in the absence of stimuli, the core of the trunk the whole woods reside in retains the wind impetus in the resin oozing from the cut limbs. Woods are wind-learning machines:

resinous gradients of twigs, widening rings, tangent curves of breeze of trees, geometries of membranes secreting the memories held

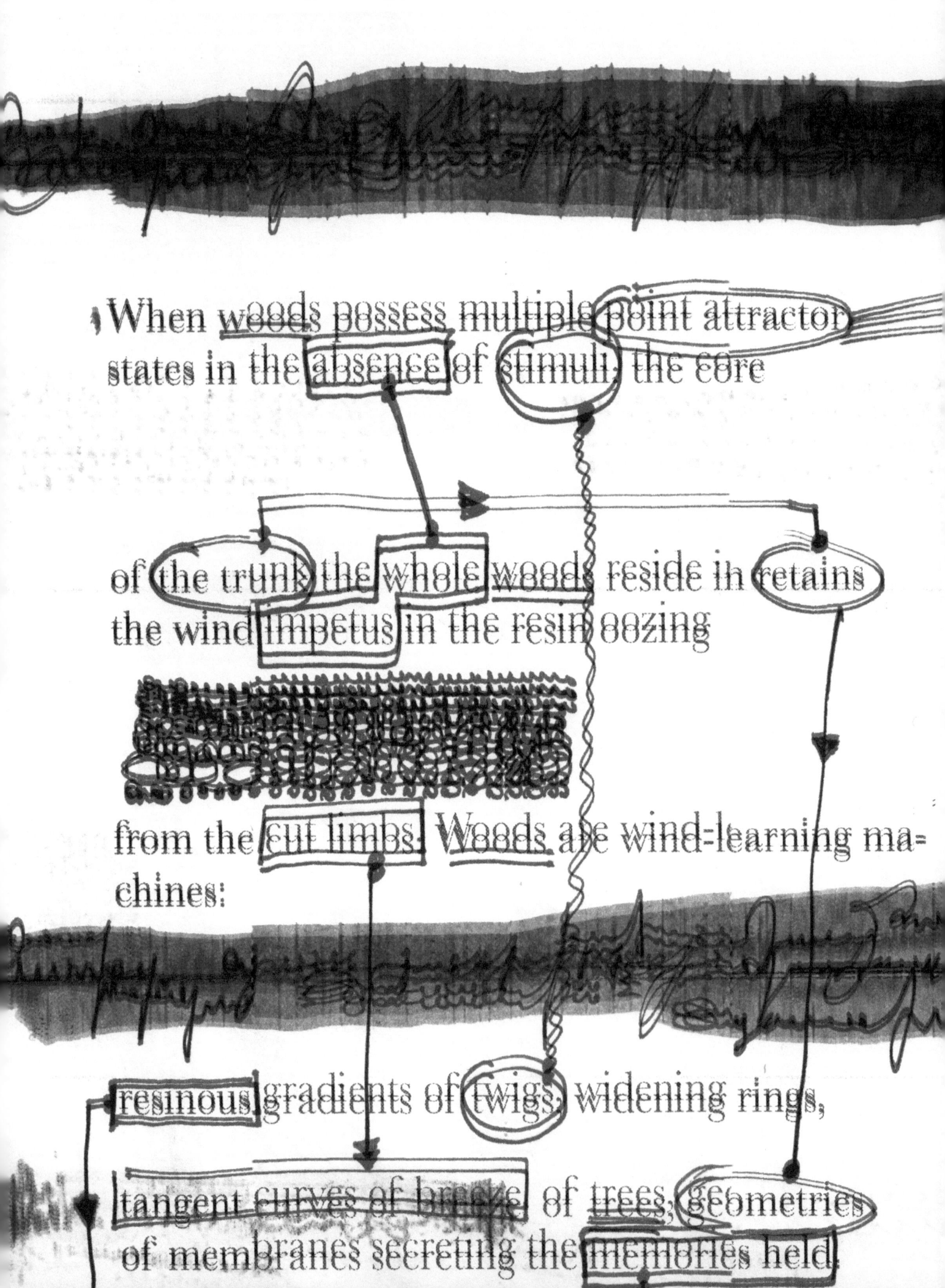

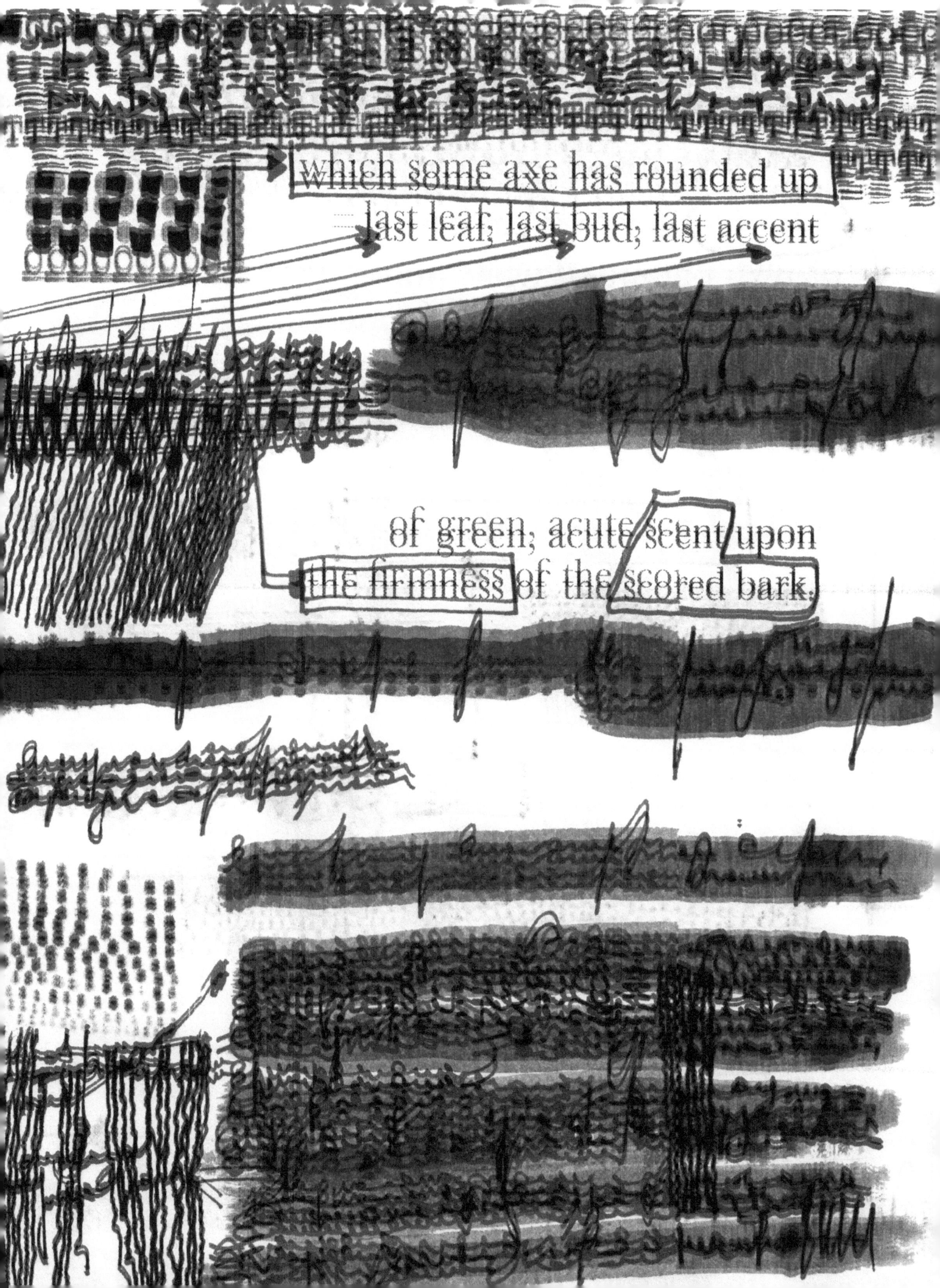

A feather from a silent nest
of owls plummets while hundreds

of leaflets expands the wind's
pitch against the needles' hiss.

Do pine cones and gravity
correlate when no air stirs?

On an undiscovered bank
of sleep, rivers sound gravels,

turn over like snakes or dead
by thirst roots in a hollow

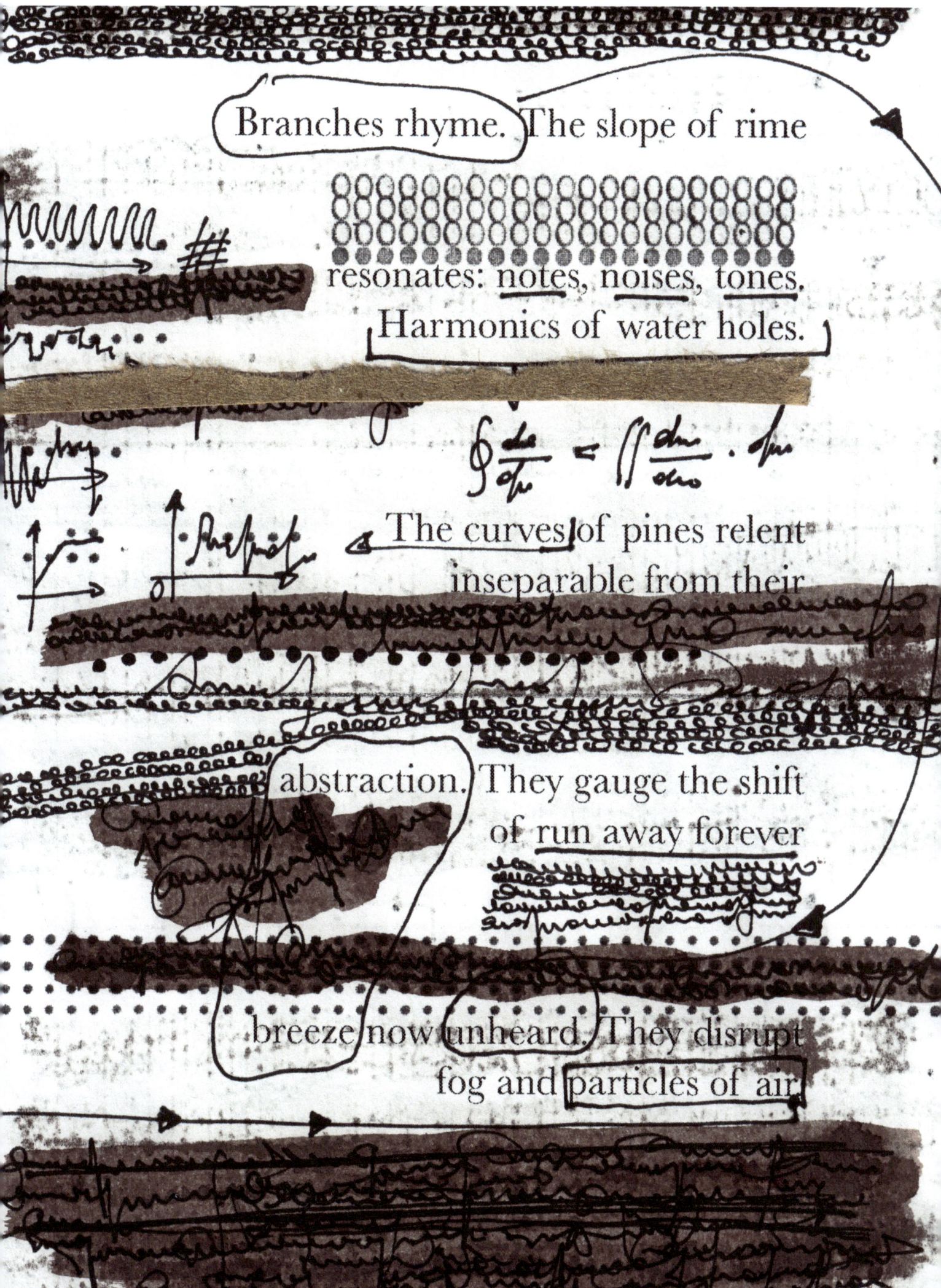

Variables nestle in tilting twigs: Leaflets align with infinitesimal greenness, model layers of careless collisions on garbled waves with peaks of instantaneous scent.

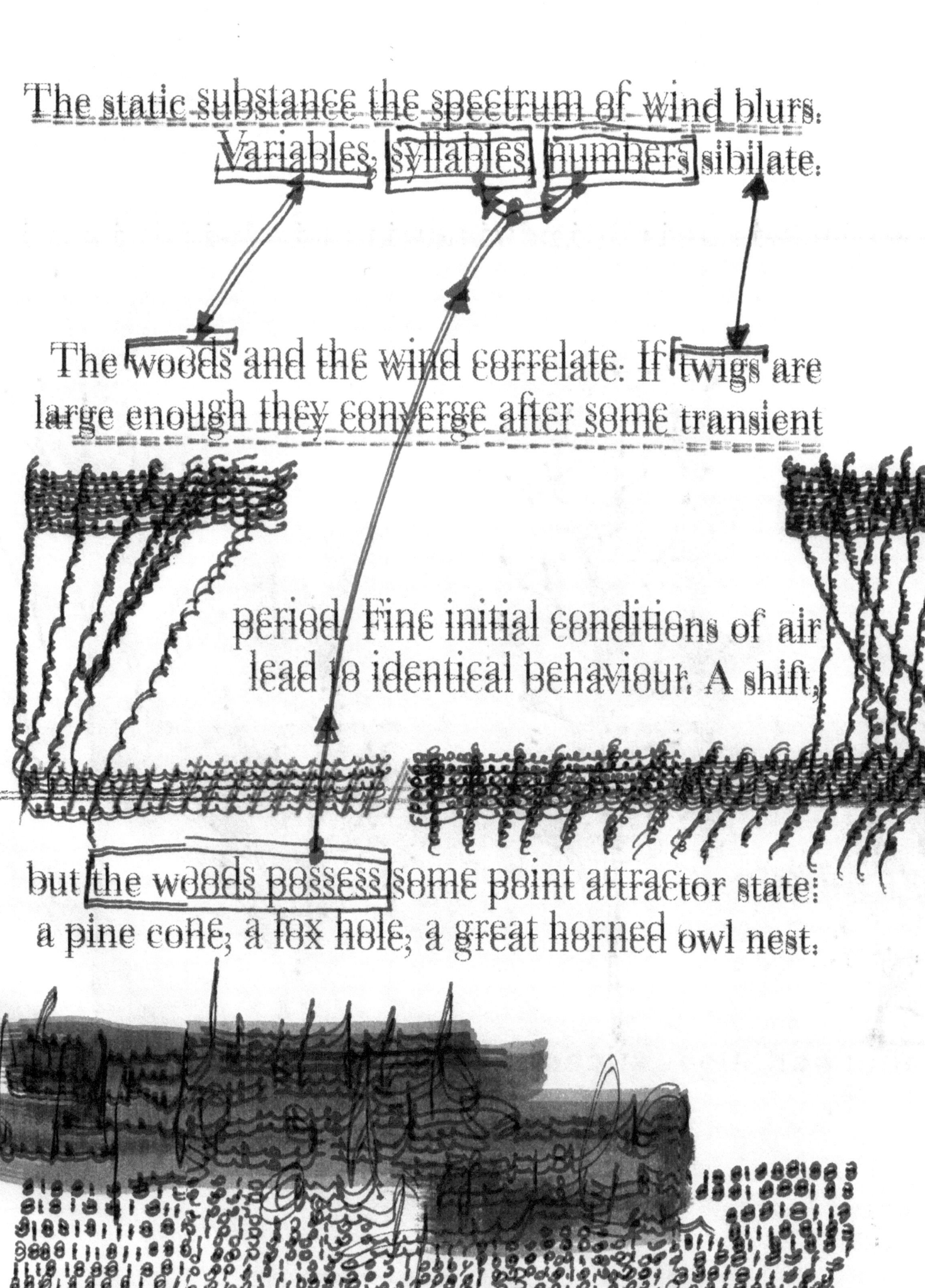

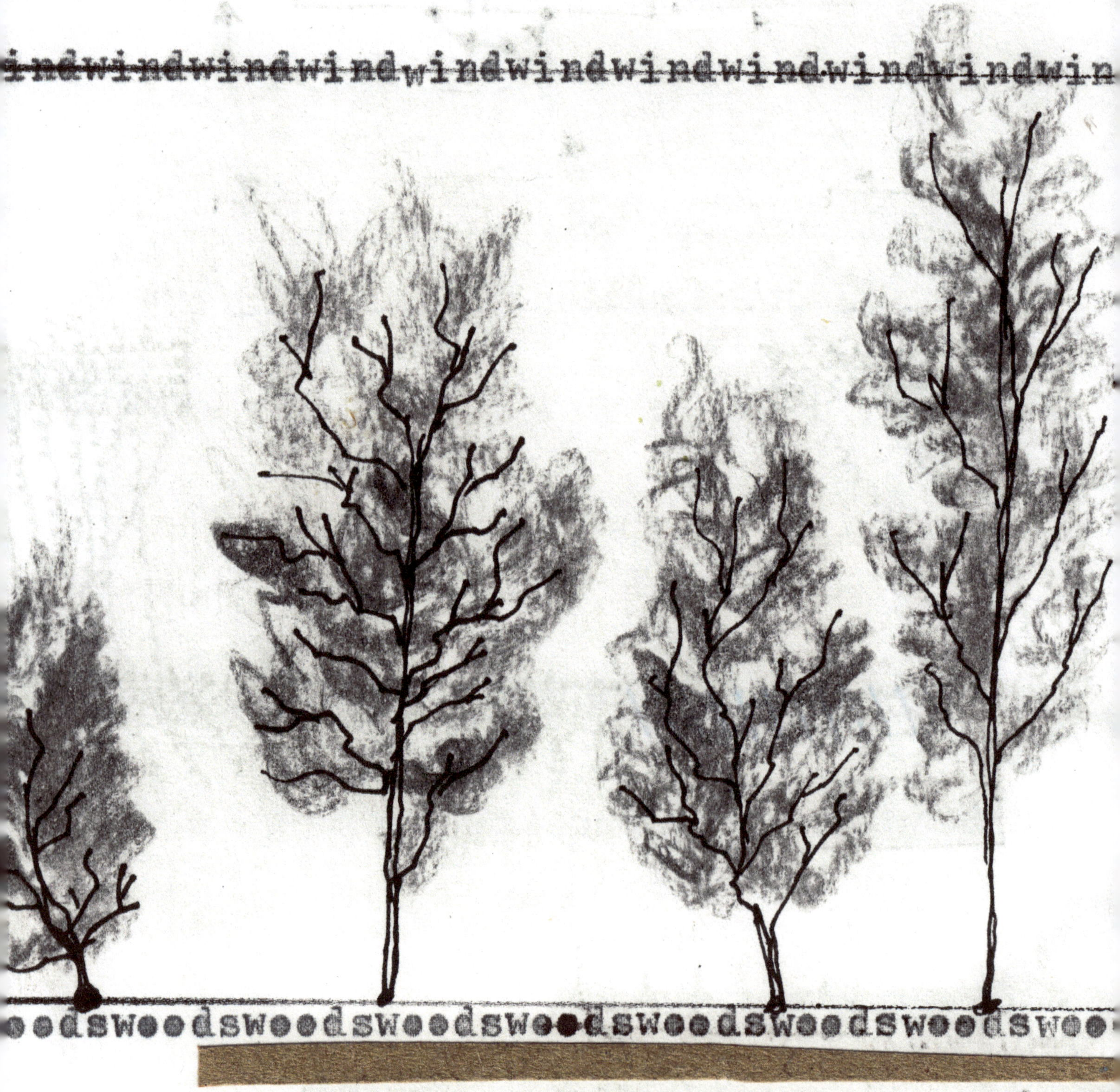
indwindwindwindwindwindwindwindwin
oodswoodswoodswoodswoodswoodswoodswoodswoo

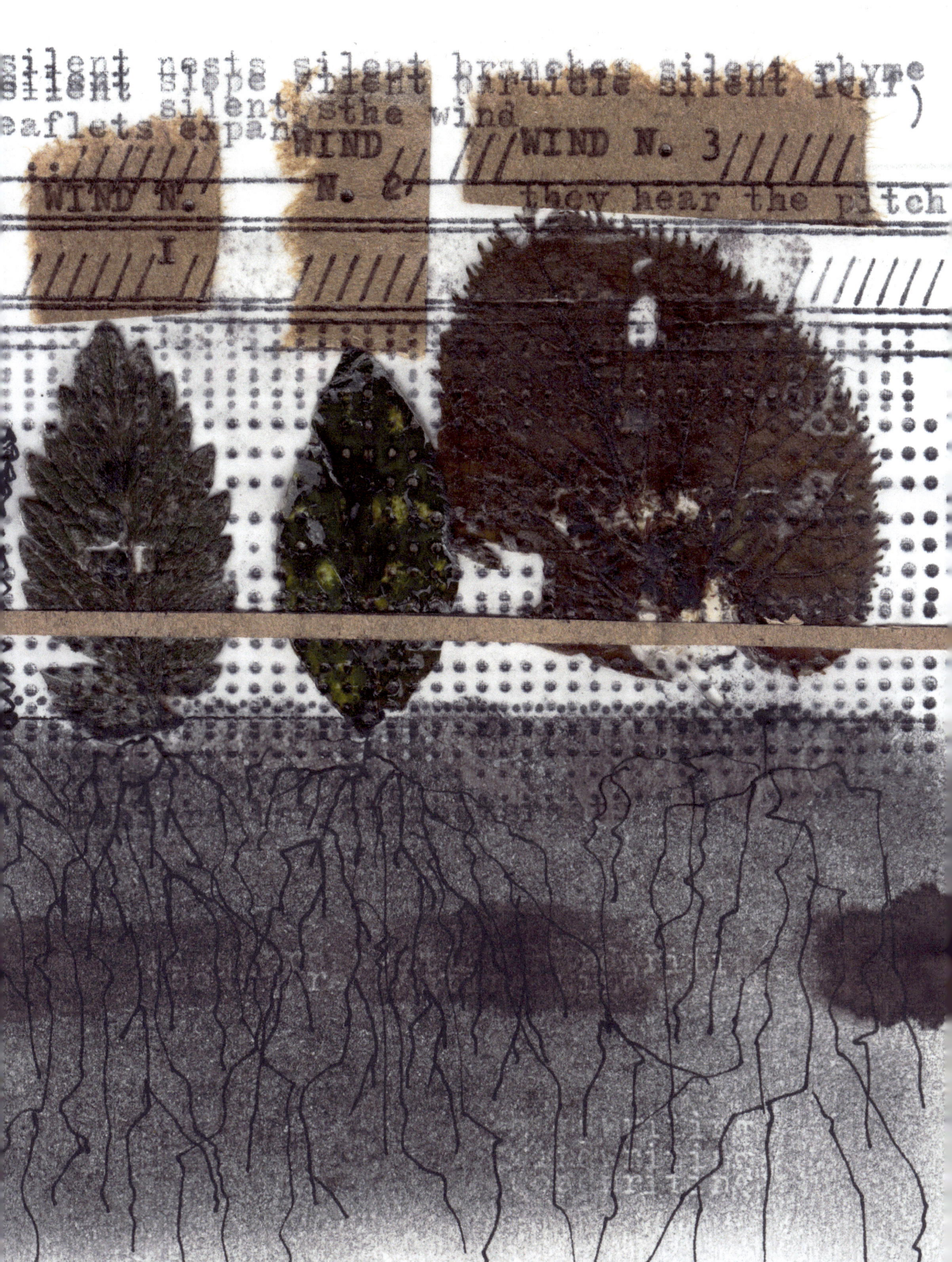

tangent curves of breeze, of trees, geometries
of membranes secreting the memories held.

Notes about a Wind to Find

1:

With a blow the wind begins
and when that blow ends it ends.

Where you hear the wind that blows
the copse grows thick, the last tree

stands where the word you die in
does not mean to. It draws dark

deciduous thoughts yet quick
to forget. The branches clot

which some axe has rounded up
— last leaf, last bud, last accent

of green, acute scent upon
the firmness of the scored bark.

The mathematics of the woods
severs vibrating needles,

reckons outspread leaves, weighs the
perennial leafing of ache

in the fresh echoes of wind,
the light pressure, that of dead

twigs, the shards of resinous
words, the hewn patterns of runes,

some numbers and all their rules.
Branches rhyme. The slope of rime

resonates: notes, noises, tones.
Harmonies of water holes.

The curves of pines relent
inseparable from their

abstraction. They gauge the shift
of run away forever

breeze now unheard. They disrupt

fog and particles of air.

A feather from a silent nest
of owls plummets while hundreds

of leaflets expand the wind's
pitch against the needles' hiss.

Do pine cones and gravity
correlate when no air stirs?

On an undiscovered bank
of sleep, rivers sound gravels,

cracked twigs shrivel up, ants
breach the universal bark.

2:

The wind is a set of continuous statements
whose size is unknown. It equates with a brain:

The vast number of variables the movements
of the woods consist of is intractable.

Nor do we know how to solve the wind, a plot
of which may converge to a particular loop.

Variables nestle in tilting twigs. Leaflets
align with infinitesimal greenness,

model layers of careless collisions on
garbled waves with peaks of instantaneous scent.

Seeming continuous variables such as barks,
membranes or surfacing root hairs get observed

under flickering leaves at the discrete times
of the wind spikes. This description requires us

to infer the pattern of hidden variables
while we observe only a sparse number of them.

Spring determines complete phase incoherence

sometime: leaves pulse in the noise of the
                              [movement
ensued from redundant wind, the density
of air drops among tall firs, beech trees and oaks.

The static substance the spectrum of wind blurs.
Variables, syllables, numbers sibilate.

The woods and the wind correlate. If twigs are
large enough they converge after some transient

period. Fine initial conditions of air
lead to identical behaviour. A shift,

but the woods possess some point attractor state:
a pine cone, a fox hole, a great horned owl nest.

If twigs diverge from each other across broad
ranges of wind while leaflets remain bounded

the woods are spreads of chaos, echoes of wind
that span spaces of hundreds of dimensions.

At the rim of the landscape, rests a dead tree,
a point on a bank of the chaos that widens.

When woods possess multiple point attractor
states in the absence of stimuli, the core

of the trunk the whole woods reside in retains
the wind impetus in the resin oozing

from the cut limbs. Woods are wind-learning
                              [machines:
resinous gradients of twigs, widening rings,

tangent curves of breeze, of trees, geometries
of membranes secreting the memories held.

3.

Temperature fluctuations set the principle
of memory formation and retrieval.

Regions of cortex and sapwood stabilize
the amount of growth in the seasonal regime.

In the wind's steady-state, in the density
of air, equally spaced needles resonate.

The miniature cycles of slow tilting loops
relent and the volume of noise sharpens

the transient of resinous gusts over slopes
of firs that smooth the uneven curve of winds.

Spruce spires set the axes, orient air layers
by gradation. The points of hewn conifers

pitch the hissing chorus of the scorched needles
discarded in the lower atmosphere.

Nothing is louder than a single axe swing
on a quiet landscape. Nothing is noisier

than the slow collisions of the snow that falls
on the fallen snow that coats drab fields of grass.

Winter confirms the monotonous friction
of a succession of clouds, wherein sparse hawks

spiral in a residual spectrum of winds.
On the rough topographies of abraded

scree slopes, where the breeze never ceases, a larch
breathes across the distance of his solitude.

4.

The plotted graph shows the patterns that characterize the wind in the observed area. Provided that an appropriate subset of data is selected, a least square approximation extracts wind parameters from vibrating needles or twigs. Their input variables need to be modelled at all relevant scales. A sufficient amount of trajectory data can also assess the wind stability in time, while probabilistic wind models can help identify tree species across different landscapes.

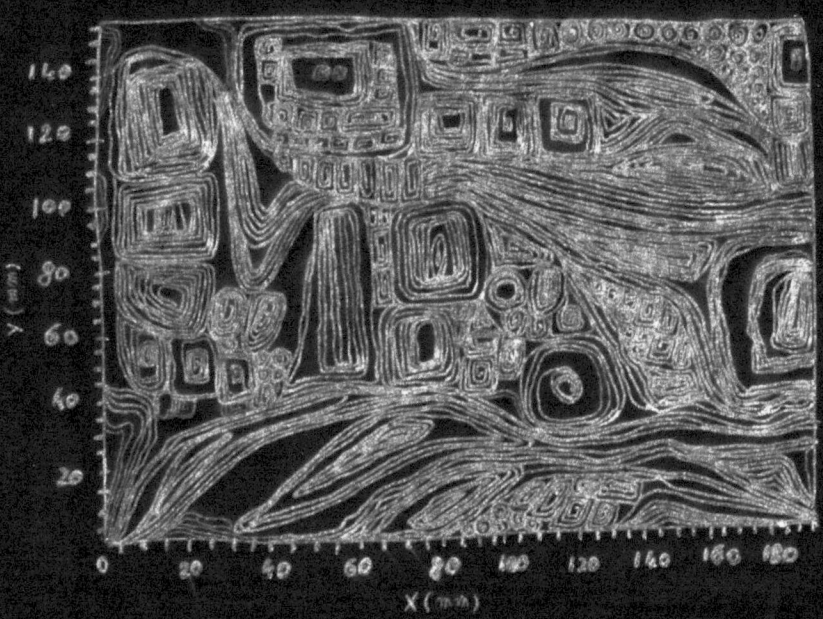

www.ingramcontent.com/pod-product-compliance
Lightning Source LLC
Chambersburg PA
CBHW051939210526
45473CB00006B/2304